GW00854660

A Newbie's Guide to Windows Phone 8

SOME PEOPLE ONLY HAVE A FEW MINUTES TO SPARE

Minute Help Press

www.minutehelp.com

Table of Contents

Introduction

If you've been paying attention to the mobile phone world lately, there are two names that will likely jump to the front of your mind: Apple and Android. While these two companies get the lion's share of the publicity (and a proportionately large number of device sales), both of them were actually *very* late to the party. Microsoft, it turns out, practically invented the smart phone. Back in the pre-iPhone days, Windows was arguably the biggest player in the nascent PDA (Personal Digital Assistant) market – helping the savviest and most forward-thinking businessmen get their work done digitally. By contrast, Apple was still trying to peddle the universally maligned Newton Message Pad.

Microsoft, by simply adapting Windows to a smaller device than the average laptop, set the stage for the mobile revolution. The glitz and glamour of the iPhone managed to distract people for awhile, but make no mistake about it: now that the majority of people worldwide do most of their day-to-day computing using smart phones, Microsoft has returned with a vengeance to stake their claim.

Building on the technological leaps made with Windows Phone 7 and 7.5, Windows Phone 8 is truly the most powerful mobile computing platform on the market today. While it might not yet have an iPhone-sized market share, it's a pretty safe bet that they'll get there pretty quickly. In fact, Microsoft has taken a bold step with Windows Phone 8: all of Microsoft's products – from Windows RT and the desktop version of Windows 8 to the software that powers the Xbox 360 – share a common aesthetic and are designed to work *together*. You won't find that on a MacBook!

Whether you've been a loyal Windows Phone user for years or you're just now growing tired of the same-old-same-old world of iOS or Android, this guide will help to make sure that you have all of the tools you need to make Windows Phone 8 your new favorite. We'll take you through Live Tiles, SkyDrive, Multitasking, Kids Corner, and a lot more – everything you'll need to make the most of your Lumia 920, HTC 8X, Samsung ATIV S, or any other Windows Phone 8 Device on the market.

Ready to get started? Let's go!

Part One: An Introduction to Windows Phone

Chapter 1: The Many Faces of Windows 8

The modern Microsoft is all about the idea of convergence: while competitors are churning out vastly different flavors of the underlying software that makes their hardware run, Microsoft is inching ever-closer to total uniformity. If you've bought a PC recently, it runs Windows 8. If you've bought one of Microsoft's new Surface tablets, it runs Windows 8. Even the Xbox 360, Microsoft's aging gaming console, has been updated to run software that's remarkably similar in functionality to Windows 8. The follow-up, rumored to be dubbed Xbox 720, will no doubt run a version of Windows 8.

This brings us to Windows Phone 8, the newest version of Windows Phone. Windows Phone 8 is very much a part of the same lineage as the rest of the current Windows stable. It's something that no other company has been able to do yet – Apple has iOS and OSX, which are so markedly different from each other that no one could *ever* confuse the two. Google has Android and Chrome OS – though they function well together, they aren't even pretending to be part of the same operating system universe. Microsoft wants to unify the user experience across *every* device in your household. And make no mistake about it: when Microsoft puts their mind to something as ambitious as this, they'll succeed.

What does this mean for you, as a new user of Windows Phone 8? It's simple: once you've mastered the basics, you'll be able to navigate *everything* else in the Windows 8 ecosystem intuitively, without having to master a bunch of new concepts and routines. Within a year or two, many businesses will have upgraded their computers to machines running Windows 8, more and more tablets will be running Windows RT (a version of Windows 8 designed to run on ARM processors), and millions of people will be using these devices alongside their trusty Windows 8 smart phones.

The point is simple, but important: whichever Windows Phone 8 device you've picked up, you've made a great decision. It's the right kind of product at the perfect time. Once you've learned your way around your new device, you'll be ready to take advantage of every Windows device on the market, mobile or not, for years to come.

If you haven't yet picked a Windows Phone 8 device, we'll offer you a quick comparison of the currently available models in the next section. Not all devices are available on all carriers, but you'll definitely be able to find the right device with minimal effort. In fact, in an effort to boost awareness (and market share), many of Microsoft's hardware partners are selling these smart phones at a pretty deep discount. You'll be able to find a Windows 8 phone with absolute top of the line specs for a lot less than you'd think.

Choosing the Right Windows Phone for You

At the time of this writing, there are around a dozen different devices that run Windows Phone 8. While some stand out from the pack for one reason or another, they all function pretty much identically. Also, every Windows 8 phone utilizes a dual-core processor and has at least 512mb of ram, which helps to make sure that they all function reasonably well.

While the rest of this guide won't devote much (if any) time to discussing the subtle differences between the devices, let's touch on a couple of different devices now – if only to help you get as much bang for your buck as you can.

There are, at present, two "flagship" Windows 8 phones on the market: The Nokia Lumia 920 and the Windows Phone 8X by HTC. They're both powered by lightning-fast 1.5 GHz processors and 1GB of ram. Both can be found (on one carrier or another) for $199, perhaps even $99 if you check around. Both are great choices and represent the high end of the market. The Lumia 920, which is the device we used for testing in this guide, has a slightly larger and higher-resolution screen. Both of these devices are available in a wide variety of fun colors:

The Lumia also boasts what's been called the highest-quality camera of any smart phone to date. While we have no real way to check that claim, we can definitely notice a quality difference between the Lumia 920 and several other devices. The camera ran circles around the iPhone 5 and the Samsung Galaxy s III in our (informal) tests. That said, the front-facing camera on the HTC 8X is significantly better than the one found on the Lumia 920. If you're planning to use your smart phone for a lot of video chatting, it's definitely something to consider. Both devices are 4G LTE capable on any carrier that supports those next-gen networks.

In the middle of the price/performance spectrum, Nokia has a few options. The Lumia 820 is very similar to its higher-end cousin, though it has a slightly smaller screen and a lower resolution. One thing the Lumia 820 has going for it – missing from *both* of the more expensive options – is a Micro SD slot. You can expand the storage significantly above the included 8GB. Of course, the Lumia 920 comes with 32GB of storage built-in, so the point could be moot.

We recommend steering clear of three low end devices, if you have a choice: the Huawei Ascend, the Samsung Ativ Odyssey, and the Nokia Lumia 620 are all sub-par devices, comparatively speaking. With the deals you can find on the super-powerful options we've already mentioned, we don't see any reason to purchase these lower-end phones.

Of course, new devices will undoubtedly be released every couple of months, so when the time comes to get a Windows 8 smart phone, do your homework. We recommend heading to **www.xda-developers.com** and searching around their Windows Phone forums – it's the place where software developers go to discuss the latest and greatest mobile devices. They'll put you on the right track.

Chapter 2: Setup

What's in the Box (and What's Missing)

*Since this guide is meant to cover an entire range of devices rather than a single smart phone, it's difficult to know for sure what you'll receive with your specific Windows phone. In our research, however, we've yet to find a Windows Phone that includes everything you truly need. Although your specific device might differ slightly, let's go over what's included with the Nokia Lumia 920, as it seems pretty representative of what you'll receive.

When you first open the box, you'll be presented with the following:

- Quick Start Guide
- Sim Card Ejection Tool
- The Device Itself
- Micro USB Cable
- Wall Charging Adapter

That's about it. Notice anything missing? There are a few things you'll want to pick up. First, and perhaps most obvious, you'll want to pick up a set of headphones, if you don't already have some. All of the Windows 8 phones have a standard 3.5mm headphone jack, so any ear buds you have lying around will do the trick. Of course, you can find several decent options from any electronics retailer for less than ten dollars.

You'll also want to pick up a protective case for your device, especially if you're the kind of person who doesn't treat their cell phone gently. Although most of the Windows 8 phones are pretty tough, you can never be too careful. We recommend heading to Amazon or eBay for a custom-designed case. While you're there, pick up some screen protectors – there's nothing worse than a shiny new phone with a scratched up screen.

You might find some (or all) of these items available at the local cell phone store where you purchased the device, but we'd like to caution you against that. Most of these items are *ridiculously* overpriced at cell phone stores. When a store charges $14.99 for a single screen protector – the very same one available in a three pack for $.99 on eBay – it's definitely a case of "That's how they get you!"

The Initial Setup

Now that you've got your Windows 8 phone in hand, it's time to run through the initial setup of the device. Unlike the different configurations you'll find on various Android devices, every Windows 8 phone is identical when it comes to setup and basic functionality, so the setup instructions won't vary at all from one Windows phone to the next.

To get started, find the power button for your device and press it. If you're having trouble locating it, there will be a diagram in the box.

> **Most Nokia devices – including the Lumia 920– will have a power button located around halfway down the right side, while some devices from other manufacturers – like the HTC 8X – will have a power button along the top:*

Once you've turned the device on for the first time, you'll be greeted with a screen that looks something like this:

Just tap the 'Get Started' button along the bottom right to continue. The next screen will be the 'Language' screen. Choose from several different languages, but note that the rest of the setup (and the device itself!) will proceed in the language you've chosen. So don't choose French for fun.

From here, you'll be taken to the Windows Phone 'Terms of Use' page. You'll need to tap the 'Accept' button in the lower right hand corner after thoroughly reading their terms and privacy policy. Consult with an attorney to make sure that you understand your rights and restrictions.

We're kidding. It's boilerplate legal stuff. Just tap 'Accept' and move on.

From here, we actually begin the setup process. You'll be presented with a screen offering you a choice between 'Recommended' settings and 'Custom' settings. The 'Recommended' settings are fine (and you can change them at any time after setup is complete), but feel free to check out the options by tapping 'Custom' and taking a look:

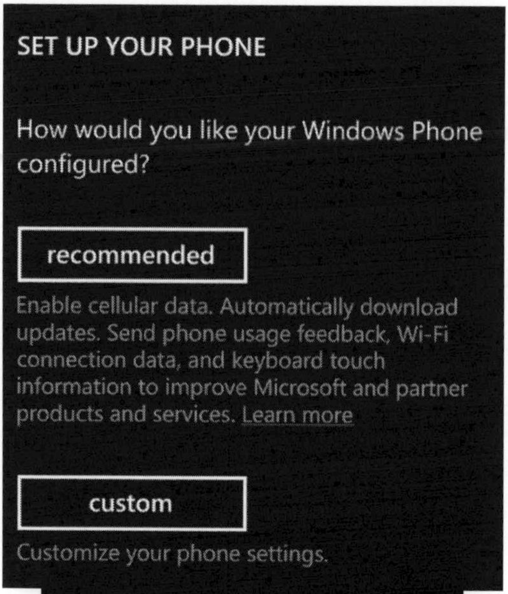

SET UP YOUR PHONE

How would you like your Windows Phone configured?

recommended

Enable cellular data. Automatically download updates. Send phone usage feedback, Wi-Fi connection data, and keyboard touch information to improve Microsoft and partner products and services. Learn more

custom

Customize your phone settings.

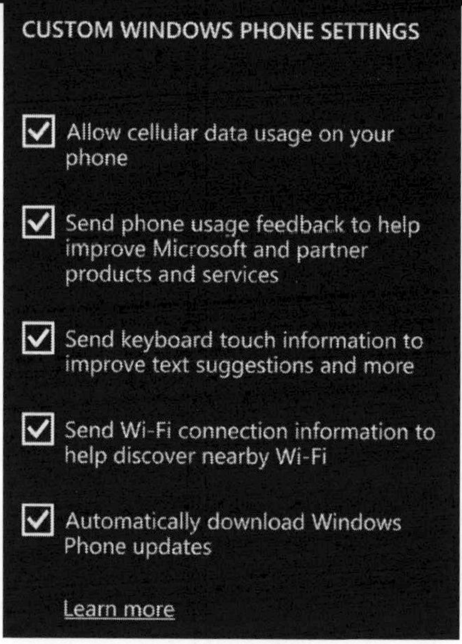

CUSTOM WINDOWS PHONE SETTINGS

☑ Allow cellular data usage on your phone

☑ Send phone usage feedback to help improve Microsoft and partner products and services

☑ Send keyboard touch information to improve text suggestions and more

☑ Send Wi-Fi connection information to help discover nearby Wi-Fi

☑ Automatically download Windows Phone updates

Learn more

As you can see, none of the available options are exactly scary. If you're the paranoid type, tap 'Learn More' to find out exactly what each setting does, and then uncheck any of the boxes you're uncomfortable with. Once you've done that, tap 'Next' to continue. Otherwise, just tap 'Previous' and then tap 'Recommended' on the screen we just left.

At this point, you'll be asked to sign into your Microsoft account. If you've ever used Windows Messenger, bought something from Microsoft.com directly, or if you own an Xbox 360, you already have a Microsoft account. If not, you'll want to create one. Thankfully, this is super easy to do:

As you can see from the above illustration, all you need to do is tap 'Create one' to get started with a new Microsoft account or tap 'Sign in' to use an existing account.

Of course, there's always the option to skip this step (which you'd do by tapping 'Sign in Later' at the bottom of the screen), but we really recommend doing it now. You don't be able to buy any apps or back up your device with SkyDrive without an account.

If you opt to create a new account, the next screen will allow you to create one using any email address you'd like. This comes in especially handy for people who are tied to their email address and don't want to deal with the hassle of creating an entirely new one. In our case, we used a Gmail address we've been using for years with no problem at all.

Once you've signed in to your Microsoft account, you're almost done. The next screen will allow you to choose your region and time zone settings. Once you've done that, tap 'Next' to continue. You'll then be asked if you want to automatically back up your device data: this includes photos, text messages, and phone settings. Again, if you're the paranoid type, you might want to tap 'Not Now', but Microsoft is one of the most secure companies in the world when it comes to user data, so there's really no reason to be dubious.

Once that's finished, you're all set. The phone will take a few more minutes to finish the setup on its own. Be patient and let it do its thing:

SETTING UP YOUR PHONE

A few more apps still need to finish installing. It should just take another moment or two.

 That's it. Now that we've finished setting the device up for the first time, let's dig a little deeper and begin exploring everything you can do with Windows Phone 8.

Part Two: Getting Started With Windows Phone 8

Chapter 3: Navigating the Phone

Now that we've finished with the setup, you've been thrust into the Windows Phone world. With no roadmap in sight, this might all seem a little confusing. Don't be scared – we'll start with the basics and move on from there. Let's start by learning all the gestures you'll need to know to interact with the device.

Ready? Let's do this!

First Things First: Touch Screen Navigation and Gestures

*Since touch-enabled devices are incredibly commonplace nowadays, people in tech circles often take the ability to effectively navigate them for granted. While many of you – possibly even a majority of you – already understand pretty much everything there is to know about touch screen gestures, we've included a little tutorial for the uninitiated. That said, if you've been using smartphones and/or tablets for any length of time, you can probably just give this section a quick once-over before moving on to the, shall we say, meatier portions of this guide.

Aside from the physical buttons relegated to volume control and turning the device on and off, you'll be navigating your way around your new Windows phone pretty much exclusively by touch. Touch screens are a great technological leap – making actions that used to take an annoyingly complex series of button presses as simple as tapping the screen – but there are a few key gestures you'll have to learn to use your phone effectively. Let's go through them one-by-one.

Tapping – A tap is a quick press of an item on your phone's screen, similar to pressing and releasing a key on a keyboard. This is probably the most common way to interact with your phone. By tapping, you can open apps, click links in the web browser, and a host of other things we'll discuss in this guide. Think of it as a click on your desktop or laptop mouse.

Double Tapping – Tapping twice in the same spot in rapid succession is referred to as a double tap. This is primarily used for zooming in on an item, especially web pages and maps. Think of it as a double click on your desktop or laptop mouse.

Tap and Hold - Tapping and then leaving your finger on the screen is known as a tap and hold. This generally brings up what's referred to as a 'context menu' of options relating to what you've selected. We'll use this gesture in a lot of places, most notably to customize the Start Screen in the next section. Think of tapping and holding as a right click on your desktop or laptop mouse.

Left or Right Swiping – Swiping is done by placing your finger anywhere on the touch screen and quickly moving it to the right or left. This is done to quickly scroll through menus and pages.

Up and Down Swiping – This is the same action as left or right swiping, but done vertically. It's useful for scrolling quickly through a web page or document.

Panning – Panning is a more controlled version of swiping. To pan, just put your finger on the screen and *gently* move it in the direction you'd like to go. This is useful for moving to a more precise location in a web page or document.

Pinching and Zooming – In order to get a better look at an item, it's sometimes necessary to zoom in. to do this, place your thumb and index finger on the touch screen and make a spreading motion on the object you'd like to zoom. To make an item smaller, make the opposite motion, moving your thumb and index finger closer together. This is very useful for working with documents, maps, web pages, photos, and even emails.

That's it for touch screen gestures. Piece of cake, right? Now that we've learned *how* to interact with the device, let's take some time and get acquainted with the Start Screen.

The Start Screen

The **Start Screen** is the default 'Home' screen of your Windows smart phone. Everything starts here. Every current version of Windows uses the same basic interface. Dubbed 'Metro', the layout and functionality of your Start Screen is simple, but full of endless customization options. Basically, it works like this: each of these little squares that you see can be resized, rearranged, or even removed. New squares can be created to represent everything from apps to contacts. Everything you use can be placed *exactly* where you want it.

These squares are called **Live Tiles**, and they've earned that name for a simple reason: they are capable of displaying real-time information. An example of this would be the "Groupon" tile on the left – notice how it displays a currently available deal? This Live Tile cycles through all of the currently available deals in the popular digital coupon app. It's displayed right on your Start Screen without you ever having to open the app itself.

The process of adding a tile to the Start Screen is referred to as **Pinning.** You can pin all kinds of things to the Start Screen, including contacts, specific map locations, group text messages, photo albums, and a whole lot more.

Before we really get around to customizing the Start Screen, however, let's backtrack a little bit and discuss the navigation buttons that you'll find at the bottom of your screen:

The Three Buttons

The most obvious way you'll be navigating around your Windows phone is by using the three on-screen buttons at the bottom of your device. These buttons serve several important functions, so let's go over them one by one, from left to right.

Back – All the way to the left of the screen, you'll find the Back button. By tapping the button once, you'll move back on screen from your current location – all the way back to the Start Screen. For example, if you're browsing a website, tapping this button will take you to the last visited page. If you're within an app, pressing this button will take you back one step within the app or – if heading back one time will take you out of the app – take you back to whatever you were doing before you opened the app. Once you've been taken back to the Start Screen, tapping the button will take you back to the last thing you did beforehand.

That's not the only thing the back button is used for. It also doubles as an 'app switcher', meaning you can tap and hold the button to bring up a list of *all* the apps you currently have open. From there, tapping any of the apps listed will bring you back to it. Swiping from right to left will take you through all of the apps, represented by smaller versions of the app's current screen:

■ **Start** – In the middle, you'll find the Start button. This is pretty much the same as the 'Home' button on an iPhone or Android smart phone. Pressing this button will take you back to the Start Screen, no matter where you are on the device.

Just like with the Back button, the Start button also pulls double duty. Tapping and holding Start will activate the "Speech" function of the device, which we'll go over a little later in this guide.

🔎 **Search**— The Search Button is probably the most helpful of all. Tapping it from *anywhere* will take you straight into Bing, Microsoft's Google-like search engine, where you can search for pretty much anything and find actionable results in an instant.

Pinning and Resizing Apps

Now that we've learned a little bit about it, we can start customizing our Start Screen. Let's start by exploring how to do two of the most common tasks: pinning an item and resizing.

To get started with pinning an item to the Start Screen, we'll first have to find an item to pin. We'll discuss pinning games, maps, websites, music, and contacts in their respective sections, but for the time being, let's pin one of the apps already on our phone to show you how it's done.

To take a look at all of your apps, just swipe from right to left on the Start Screen to bring up the app list. The list will look something like this:

For this example, we're going to pin the built-in calculator app to the Start Screen. To do this, simply tap and hold the calculator icon until a context menu comes up. You'll be given a menu option to 'pin to start', which will look like this:

Tap the menu item to pin it. Once you've done that, you'll be taken to the app's new location on the Start Screen. From here, you can re-size it by tapping the arrow on the bottom, or remove the app from the Start Screen by tapping the remove icon on the top right. Some items have several sizes to choose from, but in the case of the calculator app, we've only got two options:

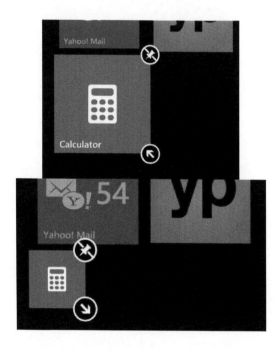

Tap the arrow a few times to see how many size options you have. Bear in mind that some of the Live Tiles will only show you data if they are medium or large size.

You can also move the pinned item wherever you'd like to on the Start Screen by using your finger (in the panning motion we discussed earlier) to drag it wherever you want it placed. Once you've settled on size and placement, just tap the Start button to finalize it.

That's it for adding apps to the Start Screen. Adding other kinds of content is just as easy, but we'll show you when we get there. For now, let's expand our customization efforts to include a little color.

Customizing: Colors and Themes

One of the most underused options in traditional desktop Windows, Microsoft has always allowed for a great deal of customization in their products. While most folks using Windows 7, Vista, or XP opt to keep everything that default shade of blue, Windows 8 – especially the smart phone version – practically begs you to change it up. It's a super easy thing to do, and goes a long way toward making your Windows 8 phone truly your own.

To get started with changing colors and/or themes, swipe left from the right side of the Start Screen to bring up the App List. Scroll down to the item labeled 'Settings' and tap it:

Once you've done that, you'll be taken to the settings menu. We'll go over it in detail later in this guide, but – for now – just find the menu item labeled 'Theme' and tap it. It should be the second from the top, right below 'Ringtones + Sounds':

Once you're inside the theme settings, you have a few options. There are two different background types: light and dark. Beyond that, you have twenty-five or so background colors to choose from. Experiment with different combinations until you find something you like. Here are just two examples of the same Start Screen in two color combinations, dark/brown on the left and light/steel on the right:

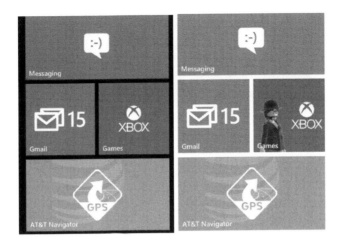

On most phones, choosing a dark background can have a positive effect on battery life. If you ever notice that your phone's battery doesn't last as long as you think it should, try switching to a dark background. It's also – subjectively, on our part – a little bit easier on the eyes.

Contacts, Phone, and the People Hub

While in recent years we've grown accustomed to using our smart phones for pretty much everything *except* phone calls, you may want to place one from time to time. You'll also probably want to keep up with your friends and loved ones via text messaging and social media, right? Thankfully, Microsoft has put pretty much all of this stuff under a single banner called the People Hub.

The People Hub is where all of your contacts are kept. It's also where you'll do the bulk of your Facebook/Twitter/LinkedIn and everything else social. Microsoft has a pretty awesome way of connecting all this stuff together, but first we'll need to get your contacts onto the phone.

If you've ever had a smart phone before, importing your contacts is pretty easy. Windows Phone 8 will automatically sync up your contacts from any of the following account types: Hotmail, Outlook, or Google. If you're coming from an iPhone, you'll have to back up your contacts to one of these services. Thankfully, there are a ton of apps in the Apple App Store that make this easy. Just search for 'contacts backup' in the App Store's search field.

To directly add an email account to sync your contacts (as well as calendars and email), first head to the app list by swiping right to left on the Start Screen. From there, find the menu item labeled 'People' and tap it.

>   *The People Hub may already be located on your Start Screen by default, so you can also tap there. In any event, it's a good idea to add it to the Start Screen as soon as possible.*

It'll look pretty empty at the moment, since we haven't yet imported any contacts. Near the bottom of the screen, you'll find three icons that look like this:

The plus sign is used to manually add a contact, while the search button next to it is meant for searching through existing contacts. To begin importing your contacts, tap the icon represented by the three small dots. Once you've done that, tap the 'settings' menu entry. Once there, you'll be greeted with this:

Find your email account type and enter the information in the appropriate boxes. Once you've done that, check the boxes labeled 'sync' for everything you'd like synced: contacts, calendars, and email. After a few moments, your People Hub should be populated with all the contacts from your email account. If you've got multiple email accounts, repeat the process. Don't worry about duplicate contacts – Windows Phone 8 is really good at weeding them out automatically, and if they miss one, it's a simple fix.

Once you've added your basic contacts, now would be a good time to add your social media accounts. Microsoft will automatically connect your Facebook friends, LinkedIn connections, and Twitter follows to your contacts. Adding these accounts will allow your contacts to display all the most recent social media updates, and allow you to post, email, text, tweet, or call right from the contact. This basically turns the People Hub into a one stop shop for all of your contacts.

Once you've added your contacts and social networking accounts, take a look around the People Hub by swiping left and right. You'll notice four sections, each with a specific purpose:

- **What's New** – This is a collection of all the most recent updates from all of your contacts and their social media profiles. You can 'Like' and comment on Facebook updates and photos right from here by tapping the appropriate button. You can also "Retweet" by tapping the appropriate button on Twitter updates.

- **Recent** - This is a quick action list of all the contacts you've recently viewed or contacted.
- **Together** – This is where your contact groups and rooms reside. This is more of an advanced concept that we'll get into in detail later in this guide.
- **All** – This is your contact list in its entirety. Scroll through and tap a name to be taken to a specific contact.

As you can see from the above illustration, there's a lot more to a contact than a phone number. There are actually four sections to each contact, accessed by swiping the same way you did in the People Hub view.

- **Profile** – Here is where you'll find all of the information about your contact. This will include links to connect with the contact in a number of different ways: You can write on a

Facebook Wall, send a text message, call, email, or even do an @mention on Twitter. If your contact allows location data, you can even find a map to their house from here!

- **What's New** – You'll find status updates specific to the chosen contact here.
- **Photos** – This is where all of your contact's social media photos are stored. You can browse through them without ever leaving the people hub.
- **History** – This, as the name implies, contains all of your recent history with the contact. Phone calls, texts, Facebook posts, etc. are all kept here.

From within the contacts view, you'll also find three icons toward the bottom of the screen:

The one on the left will allow you to pin the contact to your Start Screen. The middle icon will allow you to link the contact to any other contact in the People Hub, which is useful for unifying any accidental duplicate contacts. The icon on the right will allow you to edit any and all of the information contained in the contact, useful if your contact changes phone numbers or adds a new email address, etc.

Even though these actions are all available from within the People Hub, you can also call or text using the separate Phone and Messaging apps, which you'll find in the App List. You'll need to use the apps to call or text numbers that aren't yet in your contacts.

While looking through the 'All' section of the People Hub, you probably noticed your own picture at the very top of the list, a little larger than all of the others. This isn't an accident. This is what's known as the 'Me Card' and it's where you will post your own updates to Facebook, LinkedIn, and Twitter. It's a convenient solution, and it's probably worth pinning to your Start Screen. To do that, just tap your Me Card and then tap the 'Pin to Home' icon near the bottom of the screen. If you'd like to change the photo assigned to your 'Me Card' it's as simple as tapping the profile picture twice.

Of course, you can opt out of adding all this social networking functionality to your phone. The Microsoft App Store has separate apps for Twitter and Facebook if you'd rather keep your social networking stuff sequestered from your contacts.

So that's People Hub in a nutshell. Let's dig a little deeper now and discuss one of the most important things you'll be doing with your Windows 8 phone: browsing the web.

Internet Explorer

For web browsing, a mobile version of Microsoft's Internet Explorer 10 is included with every Windows phone. It's a full-featured web browser, and it really gives other mobile browsers (Apple's Safari and Google's Chrome) a run for their money. Its biggest strength is in its simplicity. There are just a few settings to go over.

To get started with Internet Explorer, find the icon on your Start Screen or within the App List and tap it. You'll be taken to the Internet Explorer interface, which will look something like this:

Notice that the address bar is located at the bottom, instead of the typical top of the page location. You'll do all of your navigation from here. To go to a specific website, just tap the address bar to bring up the onscreen keyboard.

As you type, Internet Explorer will attempt to guess what you're looking for. Often, you'll only need to enter a few letters before the website you'd like to access pops up. In this example, we began typing in the address for the popular music website Pitchfork.com. We only needed to enter the first three letters before the correct suggestion popped up. When you see your suggestion, just tap it to be taken to that page.

To the left of the address bar, you'll find a button. By default, this is the reload/stop button. Press it to reload the website, which is useful if you encounter errors, or you're on a page that's being regularly updated. During a website's loading, you can also tap this button to stop the website from accessing a site. This is useful when things begin taking too long, or upon encountering errors.

To the right of the address bar, you'll find the familiar three dots icon. Tap here to access the more advanced actions:

From this menu, you can open (and access) multiple Internet Explorer windows, which are called tabs. You can also access recent websites and a list of your favorites (which are chosen by tapping 'add to favorites' from this very menu). You can also share any page you're currently on via email, text, or social networks. You can also pin individual web pages to the Start Screen by tapping 'Pin to Start'.

Toward the bottom of this menu, you'll find an option labeled 'Settings.' Tap here to bring up the settings menu:

- *Website preference* – While many websites offer mobile versions of their content designed for phones, Internet Explorer offers you the option to just view the full version of any site. IE is powerful enough that mobile versions aren't all that necessary.

- *Use address bar button* for – While we just discussed the default behavior of the button to the left of the address bar, you can change it by tapping here. In addition to stop/refresh, you can use that button to access favorites, or bring up a list of your currently open tabs.

- *Delete history* – As you're probably already aware, web browsers save some information about you every time you access a website. Anything from files, visit times, or even passwords are stored within the browser. Tap here to delete that stuff at any time.

- *Privacy Statement* – This is just a shortcut to the privacy statement we read and acknowledged when setting up the device. Our guess is it's here for legal reasons.

- *Advanced Settings* – This area contains all of the complex settings that you probably won't need to mess with. From here, you can stop the collecting of cookies, turn off location access, and change the default search provider. If you plan to change any of these settings, take a look at some additional info by tapping 'Learn about these settings' at the bottom of the page.

As we discussed earlier, you can zoom in and out of web pages with ease by double tapping or using the pinching/zooming gesture.

The Camera and the Photos Hub

One of the greatest things about *any* smart phone is the camera functionality. Billions of photos are taking using smart phones, and entire companies – Instagram and Flickr chief among them— dedicated to editing and storing this new world of constant snapshots.

Windows Phone 8 not only includes this functionality, it *excels* at it. All Windows 8 smart phones have a dedicated camera button, something most other smart phones lack.

Consult the 'Quick Start' guide for your specific device to find out where it is, but you can generally find the button on the same side of the phone as the volume buttons.

To get started with the camera, simply press the dedicated camera button to open the camera app. From there, you'll be greeted with the viewfinder screen, which will look like this:

There are quite a few icons here, but don't worry – it's actually incredibly simple. To take a photo, you can do one of two things: Press the camera button halfway down to focus, then all the way down to snap the picture. You can also tap the screen to focus. Removing your finger from the screen will snap the picture.

On the right, starting from the top, the icons are:

- Advanced settings
- Turn on/off Video Mode
- Front-Facing Camera
- Flash on/off/auto
- Change lenses

To view the picture you just took, tap the left-facing arrow on the top of the screen. This will take you to the camera roll. Continue to swipe left to see all of the pictures you've taken. Windows phone includes robust editing and sharing functions, all without ever leaving the camera. As an example, we took a quick picture of our dog, and then set about editing it by tapping the three dots:

As you can see, we have several options. We can share the photo to any of our connected accounts:

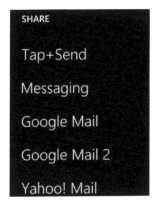

We can also delete it entirely, use it as our lock screen picture, or edit it. Since there is a big blue shopping bag in the picture, we'll opt to crop that out by tapping 'edit' and then 'crop'. We can also apply an automatic brightness fix and rotate the picture directly from here, just by tapping the appropriate button.

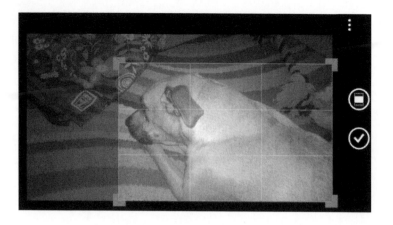

The Lenses button is another interesting concept. Rather than constantly switching to *other* camera apps like you would with the iPhone or an Android smart phone, Microsoft has allowed developers to work *with* the camera and with each other. Basically, you can download a 'lens' that will – for example – help you create a panorama shot. Instead of exiting the default camera and opening a panorama camera application, you can get to it in one step by tapping the 'lenses' button.

From there, any picture you take with a 'lens' app will automatically save to the camera roll. Some lenses also add editing functionality to the editing area of the camera roll. To check out some lenses, just tap the lenses button and poke around that section of the Windows App Store, which we'll discuss a little later in this guide.

That's pretty much all there is to it. If you'd like to take a video, just tap the video button and press the camera key to begin taking the video. Press it again to stop. You won't have the editing capabilities that you do with photos, but you can share to a number of places directly from the camera, just as you would with your pictures.

The advanced menu (the three dots, again) contains things like ISO and scene settings. We found that we were able to get great shots without messing with these settings, but if you're an experienced camera person, it's worth a look.

The Photos Hub, accessible from the App List or the Start Screen, is where your photos will be placed. From here, you can share the photos you've taken, look at the photos your contacts have taken, and directly access any camera-centric apps you've downloaded (which we'll discuss in the next section). This comes in handy for editing your photos on the fly, all without leaving the photos hub.

You can also sort your pictures into albums, or view them by date taken. You can also tag people in photos, and view all the photos including (or taken by) that person. The whole Photos Hub concept really must be seen to be appreciated. We think you'll spend a great deal of time here, especially if you're a photo nut like us.

Part Three: Getting More out of Your Windows Phone

Chapter 4: Pushing Your Phone to the Next Level!

Now that we've figured out our way around the device, played with a few built-in apps, and gotten ourselves comfortable, let's build on that and pay a visit to the Windows Store. While we're at it, we'll connect our Windows Phone to our PC or Laptop, which will come in handy a little later.

Ready? Let's go!

The Windows Store and the Windows Phone App

When we first set up the device, we set up a Microsoft Account to allow us to connect to two things: SkyDrive and the App Store. While there's a whole lot you can do with the device without ever downloading any third-party apps, you'll probably want to begin an apps and games collection that'll *really* show off what your device is capable of.

To get started with the Windows Store, just find the app labeled 'Store' in the App List or on the Start Screen. The first time you open the Store, you may have to re-enter your account password. Once you've done that, you'll be taken to a screen that looks something like this:

From here, you can browse for an app, game, podcast, or even music by tapping the appropriate menu item or swiping from right to left. You can also use the search button at the bottom to search for something specific. When you find something you'd like to see more information about, just tap it to bring up the app's page. The pages will look something like this:

Many of the apps and games in the Windows Store can be downloaded as 'free trials' and used for a limited amount of time, or with reduced functionality. When you come across one of those, just tap 'Try for Free' and the App will download just like any other.

Tap 'Buy' to begin the purchasing process. By default, the things you download will be charged to your cell phone bill. Don't worry, though, it's easy to change. Once you've gotten to the confirmation screen after hitting 'Buy', find the item labeled 'Add or switch payment methods' and tap it. You'll be brought to a screen where you can add a credit/debit card, a Microsoft gift card, or a PayPal account. Enter the payment method of your choice, and tap to confirm.

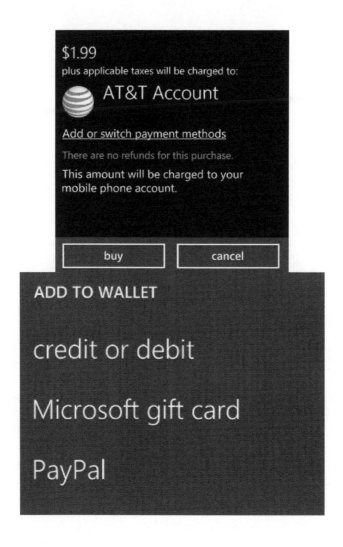

*Just an FYI: While any applications you buy will end up in
the App List, any games you buy will end up within the Xbox
Games App. They haven't disappeared!*

That's pretty much all there is to the Windows Store. We'll show
you a few of our favorite Windows Phone apps at the end of this
guide, but for now, let's turn our attention to connecting the
Windows Phone to your computer.

In the spirit of inter-connectedness, Microsoft has released an application for desktop and laptop computers that seamlessly connects your phone to your Windows 8, Windows 7, or Mac PC. The best part? You don't have to go searching for it – all you need to do is plug your phone into an available USB port.

This guide is intended for Windows PCs, but should be fairly similar to the installation on a Mac.

To get started with the Windows Phone App, go ahead and plug your phone into a desktop or laptop via the included USB cable. The familiar 'Installing Device Driver' balloon will pop out of the corner. After this automatic install, you'll be presented with a new window that will look like this:

Just click the icon labeled 'Get the Windows Phone App' to begin. From there, a web browser window will open. In the middle left of the page, you'll find a black box that looks like this:

Sync with your PC

Install or upgrade to the new and improved Windows Phone app for desktop to sync music, photos, videos, and more with your PC.

Download now

Click the link marked 'Download now' to proceed. Approve the download (if necessary) and the open the file. It's called WindowsPhone.exe. Once you've done that, follow the steps to install the program. Once you've done that, you'll go through a small preferences setup, where you can change the name of your phone and set it up to automatically sync all of your videos and photos to the computer. You can also choose to import your music, movies, and TV shows from either iTunes or Windows Media Player.

Once you've set your preferences, everything will be done for you each time you open the application. You can now access all of your pictures and videos in the default Windows library for the file type, accessible from the explorer window:

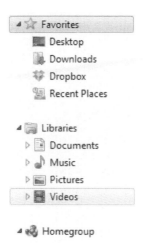

If you're not interested in using an app to get files to and from your computer, there is another easy solution. Once the drivers for your phone have been installed, you can treat the phone as if it's a hard drive. To do this, just look under the computer tab of your explorer window:

By clicking on 'Windows Phone' you'll open up the writable portion of your phone's drive, which consists of several folders:

| Documents File folder | Music File folder | Pictures File folder |
| Ringtones File folder | Videos File folder | |

To add things to your device, just drag them and drop them in the appropriate folder. To move things to your computer from the phone, drag any item *from* these folders to your computer. It's that simple.

The Music + Videos Hub

Now that we've connected our Windows Phone with our PC or laptop and synced up our music and/or videos libraries with our device, we can now take full advantage of the Music + Videos Hub. If you haven't guessed by now, this is where all your songs and videos are held. Like the Photo Hub, this is also where you'll find any music or video-related apps you might download, like Last.FM or Netflix.

To get started with the Music + Videos Hub, just find the icon labeled 'Music + Videos' either on your Start Screen or within the App List and tap on it. Once you've done that, you'll be greeted with a screen that looks something like this:

There are five sections to the Music + Videos Hub, all of them accessible by swiping from right to left. In order, they are:

- *Collection* – this is where you'll find all the music, videos, and podcasts on your device, sorted by category, then alphabetically. There's also a link to the Windows Store, where you can download more of the content you want.
- *History* – this area shows you what's playing and what's recently played. This is useful for resuming playback on things you haven't finished and creating queues and playlists.
- *New* – all the stuff you've recently added from your computer or downloaded from the store will show up here.
- *Apps* – all of your video and audio related apps will reside here.
- *Xbox* – This area is useful if you own an Xbox. You can visit the Xbox Music Store and connect with your Xbox 360 using the SmartGlass app, which we'll discuss at the end of this guide.

The Music + Videos Hub will play pretty much any video or audio file you throw at it. We used .AVI and .MP4 for video as well as .MP3, .WMA, and .WAV files for audio during our tests and playback for all of them was seamless. As an example, we copied over an episode of the television show *Shameless* to the 'Videos' folder using the Windows Explorer method above. Immediately after copying, it showed up in the app, ready to play. Tapping it immediately brought us to a widescreen playback screen:

As you can see, you're given a familiar set of controls. Pressing the play/pause button will play/pause the video. Pressing the rewind button will skip to the beginning of the file, while pressing the fast forward button will skip to the end (or the next file, if there is one). There's a scrubber bar beneath all that. Tap and hold the little white ball and move left or right to navigate forward and backward within the item.

Audio works in much the same way, except for the added ability to create playlists of your music to save for later. The process is a little convoluted, but we'll walk you through it:

- Tap the 'Music' button in the 'Collections' section. Find the artist, album, or song that you'd like to begin your new playlist with and then tap and hold it. Once the menu comes up, tap 'Add to Now Playing.' This adds the file to the 'Now Playing' queue.
- Open the 'Now Playing' queue by swiping over to the 'History' section and tapping on the item that's currently playing. Tap the song title to bring up the queue and then tap the 'Save' Button. Enter a name for the new playlist and tap the enter button on your pop-up keyboard. Your playlist will be accessible from Collection – Music – Playlists. You can also add any song you like to it now by tapping and holding on the song and then tapping 'add to [name of playlist]'.

SkyDrive

You've probably heard people discussing 'The Cloud' at some point in the last few years. It sounds amazing and ethereal, doesn't it? Well, SkyDrive is Microsoft's 'cloud' solution, an answer to other applications like DropBox and Google Drive. But what does it do? It's a lot simpler than it seems at first blush. SkyDrive is just a place to back up and store files that aren't kept on the storage that comes with your PC or phone.

Microsoft has included 7 GB of SkyDrive cloud storage free for every user. Users of cloud storage services like Dropbox or iCloud will be familiar with the concept behind Microsoft's SkyDrive, but the company's take on it is a little bit different.

Basically, SkyDrive is a folder (or group of folders) stored on the Internet, but accessible only to you and your devices. Copying a file from your computer to SkyDrive will make the file available pretty much instantaneously across all of your other SkyDrive-enabled devices.

For example, let's say you've written a document in Word on your PC. You're sitting in the living room, watching television, when you suddenly remember a paragraph or two you've forgotten to include. You can just pull the same file up on your Windows Phone and edit it without having to trudge back to your home office. The changes you make from the living room will automatically be applied to the file on your PC.

When we first set up your Windows Phone, we actually created SkyDrive account to back up our pictures and contacts. To get the most out of SkyDrive, however, we're going to have to download the standalone apps for both our computer and Windows Phone. In Windows 8 or on your Windows Phone, that's as easy as searching for the app in the App Store and downloading it. If you're using another operating system, like OSX, Windows 7, or Windows Vista, it's a little bit more complicated.

To download the application to your desktop or laptop PC, head over to **www.microsoft.com**. Once there, you'll notice a search bar in the upper right hand corner. Type 'SkyDrive' in the search bar and click search. The first result will be the SkyDrive app. Click again to download it.

Once it's downloaded, click to open the file and install it. Follow the prompts and enter your Microsoft ID and password in the fields. Make sure it's the same ID you use on your Windows Phone. That's all there is to it. You'll now have a folder in Explorer that looks like this:

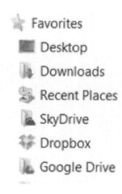

Now that you've installed the app for the desktop, go ahead and download it for your device. Just open the Windows Store by tapping in the app list or on the Start Screen and search for 'SkyDrive'. It should look like this:

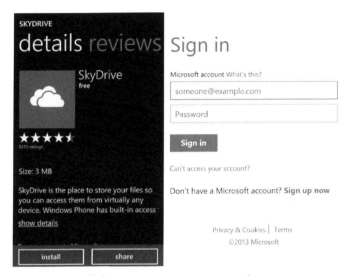

Once you've downloaded the app, find it in the App List and open it. The first time, you'll have to enter your Microsoft Account information. Once you've done that, you'll have access to SkyDrive. Copy some things over from your PC to see how it works.

As an example, we copied over the same episode of *Shameless* that we watched in the last second. It was almost instantly visible within the SkyDrive app on the phone, and tapping it opened the file within the Music + Video Hub immediately. You can do the same with all kinds of files – music, documents, pictures, and a whole lot more.

The Settings Menu

We've covered some common settings at various points in this guide, but we'd like to go over the settings menu in its entirety. Most of these things you'll never have to mess with, but it's still information you should have.

The settings menu on Windows Phone is pretty unique. When you open it, you'll see that it's split into two separate sections: System and Applications. Windows has taken every single setting from every single app (the infamous three dots) and put them in one place, which is a real timesaver. Of course, your individual apps (and their settings) will vary, so let's focus on the 'System' category. Here's the rundown, in order – from top to bottom:

- *Ringtones and Sounds* – tap here to change your ringtone and other system sounds, such as the noise you hear when receiving a text message. You can copy ringtone files directly to the device using either the Windows Phone App or the Explorer method we discussed earlier. If you don't know how to create a ringtone, we suggest heading to the excellent **www.myxer.com** and following the super easy tutorial.
- *Theme* – We discussed changing themes in part two of this guide. Check there for instructions.

- *Email + Accounts* – this is the very same 'add account' menu that we dealt with in the People Hub section of this guide.
- *Internet Sharing* – Tapping this button will allow you to share your phone's internet connection with other devices, otherwise known as 'tethering.' Consult with your cell phone provider before doing this, as many companies charge extra for the privilege.
- *Lock Screen* – This section contains all of the settings for the customizable lock screen. From here, you can add a picture as a background, and choose which (if any) information to show – like unread emails, missed calls, etc. Play around until you figure out what you like best. There are a ton of options.
- *Wi-Fi* – This section will show you all of the available Wi-Fi networks where you're currently located. You can also shut off Wi-Fi entirely from here, if you're not in range of your home (or a good public) network.
- *Bluetooth* – For those of you with Bluetooth headsets and whatnot, tap here to initiate the 'pairing' process. Windows Phone treats Bluetooth pretty well; it's a breeze to set up from here.
- *Tap + Send* – NFC (short for Near-Field Communication) hasn't really taken off yet, but most Windows Phones have the technology built-in. Similar to Bluetooth, NFC allows file transfers between devices over short distances. Turn this on or off to allow that.
- *Airplane Mode* – This turns off all the radios inside your phone, cellular, GPS, Wi-Fi, Bluetooth, and NFC. Use it when the captain (or flight attendant) says 'turn all electronic devices off.'
- *Cellular* – This area contains information about your cell phone network. It's a good idea to *not* mess with any settings here.

- *Location* -- Most cell phones have a GPS (short for Global Positioning System) built-in. This is what allows maps and other location-specific apps to know where you are. Turn this off if you don't want to allow data about your location to be collected.
- *Kid's Corner* – This is where you'll set up the awesome Kid's Corner functionality which we'll discuss in the next section.
- *Battery Saver* – This section contains an advanced setting, designed to maximize battery life. If you turn it on, your battery life will improve, but apps will only work when they're opened, meaning things like email won't come through unless checked for manually. In our experience, we found negligible difference, perhaps an extra 15 minutes of battery life.
- *Backup* – This is a shortcut to the automatic SkyDrive backup that we set up when setting up the device. If you want to change what gets backed up, this is where you'll go.
- *Date + Time* – Use this to change your clock settings.
- *Brightness* – use this to adjust the brightness settings for your screen. We recommend using 'automatic,' which will adjust periodically to changes in the brightness of your surroundings.
- *Keyboard, Language+Region, Speech* – These areas control the language settings for various functions.
- *Ease of Access* – this section contains the settings for the visual or hearing impaired.
- *Find my Phone* – This section contains settings for 'Find my Phone.' If you ever lose track of your device, you can locate it by heading to **www.WindowsPhone.com** and logging in.
- *Phone Update* – Check here periodically to see if there are any pending software updates for your phone model.

- *About* – This is perhaps the most important section of all. You'll find information about your phone, sure, but if you scroll to the bottom, you'll also find a button labeled 'Reset my Phone.' You'll want to do this if you run into any weird software glitches, plan to sell the device, or just want to start over. Keep in mind that you'll be erasing *everything*, so make sure everything you'll need is backed up before proceeding.
- *Network+* -- Contains some advanced network settings that you won't want to mess with. This is mainly there for repair people at the cell phone store.
- *Audio* – This section contains an equalizer and a couple other audio enhancements. Head here if your phone isn't sounding as good as you think it should.

That's about it for the settings menu. As we said earlier, you probably won't have to mess around with this stuff very often, but always be careful when you do. If you're unsure of something, ask your cell phone provider before making any changes.

Extra Tips and Tricks: Bing Vision and Kid's Corner

We've already done quite a bit with Windows Phone, but saying that there's still a lot to explore would be the understatement of the century. Some of this stuff is brand-specific, like the excellent augmented reality tool Nokia City Lens, while other tricks, like the built in Bing Vision scanner, might be easy to overlook. Bing Vision can scan all kinds of electronically generated codes, including barcodes, ISBNs, Microsoft Tags, and QR Codes.

For the uninitiated among you, a QR code is a unique pattern, readable by smart phones, that has *something* embedded in it. It could be a coupon, a bit of text, a link to a web page or music file – the possibilities are pretty staggering. You've probably seen them on billboards or in magazines. These QR codes look like this:

While you would typically need to download a QR code reader application, Microsoft built this functionality into the search button. To scan a QR code, just tap the search button from the Start Screen. Once you've done that, you'll be taken to the Bing search page, which will look something like this:

The icon with the eyeball on it is Bing Vision. Tap it to begin scanning and point the camera at a QR code. If you pointed it at the one above, you'll be presented with this message:

It's a neat concept, and you might be thinking that it's just a novelty. Using the very same Bing Vision app, we picked a DVD at random from the shelf and decided to scan it. Here's what came up:

Tapping the movie's poster brought us to a page with a *ridiculous* amount of information about the movie:

We were given information about where to buy it cheaply, what people think of the movie, detailed cast notes, and a bunch of other stuff – all from within the Bing Vision app. Try it out for yourself, it's almost scary.

Bing Vision is just one example of the cool stuff you can do with your Windows Phone. Let's cover one more thing before we finish up. It's called Kid's Corner. If you're a parent, this function is a godsend.

If you're ever out and about in public, say at a restaurant, and you want to keep your toddler (or tween) busy, you'll probably be tempted to hand them your smart phone so they can play a game or watch a movie. This, as anyone who's ever accidentally lost *everything* because of a curious child can tell you, is often a recipe for disaster. Still, it's a common thing: your kid wants to play Angry Birds. What do you do? Kid's Corner is your solution.

It works like this: You can set up Kid's Corner to work as a 'virtual' environment. Add some apps, games, movies, etc. to it, create a password, and open it. Hand it to your kid and they can use those apps and *only* those apps. They won't be able to exit the Kid's Corner and wreak any havoc on the rest of your phone.

To get started with Kid's Corner, go to the Settings Menu entry for it that we discussed in the last section. Tap it and you'll be greeted with this screen:

Tap 'Next' to proceed. From here, you'll be asked to choose some kid-friendly apps, videos, games, and/or music:

Add whatever you like, and then tap 'Next.' After you set a password, Windows will automatically turn Kid's Corner on. That's all there is to it. When you unlock the device, you'll be in Kid mode, which will look something like this, depending on the content you've allowed:

To exit Kid's Corner, just tap the power button. Tap it again, and you'll be back to the default lock screen. Swipe and enter the password to get back to your phone. If you want to get back to Kid's Corner, swipe from right to left on the lock screen, then swipe up. Pretty cool, huh?

Chapter 5: Must-Have Apps and Games

While we've covered a lot of built-in apps, there's a whole universe of third-party content awaiting you. We hope that you spend some time digging around the Windows Store for some cool apps and games, but in the meantime, here's a few of our favorites to get you started.

Wikipedia (free) –For the uninitiated, Wikipedia is a user-generated digital encyclopedia that has information about any topic you can possibly imagine. We like to tap random and drift from article to article for hours, learning about everything from Mexican haberdashery to equine mating habits. The Windows Phone interface is fast and simple – which is exactly what Wikipedia is supposed to be.

Angry Birds: Star Wars ($4.99) – If you've ever used a mobile device, chances are you played the original Angry Birds on it. This follow-up to the most popular video game of all time pits the loveable birds against the Empire (of pigs). Even if you're not a fan of the Star Wars movies, you *will* become addicted to this game, we pretty much guarantee it.

Netflix (free trial, then $7.99 monthly) – Netflix is the king of Internet video streaming. With an enormous catalog of award-winning films and television shows, there's always something to watch. While the Netflix application exists on a variety of platforms, the Windows Phone version is among the fastest and most intuitive we've tried. If you've never used the service before, they'll even let you try it for 30 days before charging you.

Hulu Plus (free trial, then $7.99 monthly) – The main competitor to Netflix, Hulu Plus doesn't have *quite* the level of content of its chief rival, but where it really shines is in episodes of currently airing television shows. Most of the major networks release their shows for streaming on Hulu Plus the day after they've aired, which can be really great for cord-cutters and super-busy people. Sadly, their free trial only lasts 14 days, but the desktop browser version (Hulu without the 'plus') is completely free, with a slightly more limited selection.

Reddit to Go! (free) – Reddit is the world's largest social news site. Home to millions of news junkies and witty commentators, you're sure to find a home in one of the thousands of "Sub-Reddits" about almost any topic you can imagine. There are a few different Reddit apps in the Microsoft App Store, but this one is the best by a clear mile.

IM+ (free) - If the People Hub isn't quite enough social connection for you, IM+ will definitely fulfill your requirements. Literally every single messaging platform is included here, allowing you to connect to services like Google Chat, Yahoo! Messenger, AOL Instant Messenger, ICQ, and about a dozen more.

Conclusion

Well, that's it. You've learned to navigate your way around your Windows Phone 8. We've downloaded some apps, taken some photos, set up SkyDrive, and a lot more. While you're a certified expert now, there's still plenty more to explore. We sincerely hope that your new Windows phone gives you years of enjoyment and productivity. We hope you enjoyed this guide, and we hope we've instilled in you the confidence to make this device do everything you've ever dreamed of, and then some.

Thanks for reading!

About Minute Help Press

Minute Help Press is building a library of books for people with only minutes to spare. Follow @minutehelp on Twitter to receive the latest information about free and paid publications from Minute Help Press, or visit minutehelpguides.com.

Printed in Great Britain
by Amazon.co.uk, Ltd.,
Marston Gate.